A Doctor Among the Santals

*The Autobiography of
Dr. Stephen B. Hansdak*

A Doctor Among the Santals

The Autobiography of Dr. Stephen B. Hansdak

EDITED BY

Ivy Imogene Hansdak

2012

A Doctor Among the Santals: *The Autobiography of Dr. Stephen B. Hansdak* – published by the Rev. Dr. Ashish Amos of the Indian Society for Promoting Christian Knowledge (ISPCK), Post Box 1585, 1654, Madarsa Road, Kashmere Gate, Delhi-110006.

© Author, 2012

The views expressed in the book are those of the author and the publisher takes no responsibility for any of the statements.

ISBN: 978-81-8465-212-3

Cover Illustration: Sunder Manoj Hembrom
E-mail: smanoj0876@gmail.com

Laser typeset by

ISPCK, Post Box 1585, 1654, Madarsa Road, Kashmere Gate, Delhi-110006 • *Tel:* 23866323

e-mail: ashish@ispck.org.in • ella@ispck.org.in
website: www.ispck.org.in

Dedicated to the
early missionaries of Mohulpahari—

Paul Olaf Bodding

Christine Larsen

Johannes Gausdal

Kristofer Hagen

William R. Scott

Otto Forman

Egil Ofstad

Alice Axelson

Ella Malterud

Anne Marie Sulen

Hilma Gjerde

Randi Kopperud

Contents

Acknowledgements

I begin by thanking my mother, Mrs. Alice Hansdak, without whose help this book could never have taken shape. I also thank my paternal aunts, Salomi and Euniki, who patiently answered all my questions despite old age and failing health (sadly, my aunt Euniki passed away a few months later); likewise, I thank my uncle, Hanuk Hansdak. I also thank my elder sister and brother, Eva and Christopher, for helping in their own special way.

I take this opportunity to thank my friends from Norway, particularly Elizabeth Doerdal, Egil and Kaja Ofstad, Eliza Dragoey, Heid Haugstad, Anny Saeter and Oddver Holmedal. I also acknowledge an old family friend from America, Dr. James R. Michel, whose visits to Mohulpahari were so full of fun.

I express my heart-felt gratitude to Dr. Shantidani Minz of CMC, Vellore, for her boundless generosity; not only did she help me with the editing work but also welcomed me into her family at Vellore. I also thank Marine Carrin and Harald Tambs-Lyche for writing the Introduction and Anand Mahanand, for the Foreword. Likewise, I thank Sunder Manoj Hembrom for his creative contribution.

Finally, I apologize for any error that might exist in my brief chronicle of Santal Christian history. I know there are many people whose involvement with the Santal Parganas is more grounded than my textual ones.

I wish them all a bright future!

Ivy Imogene Hansdak

Foreword

The narrative, *A Doctor among the Santals: The Autobiography of Dr. Stephen B. Hansdak*, is a carefully conceived work compiled by his scholar daughter, Ivy Imogene Hansdak. It has been placed in the context of the time and space in which Dr. Stephen Hansdak lived and worked. It is aptly stated by Ivy Hansdak that this narrative not only sheds light on her father's life but also provides glimpses of the social history of the Santhals during the late nineteenth and early twentieth centuries. It captures the life of Dr. Stephen Hansdak, who came from a silent and obscure village of the Santal Parganas but managed to reach the heights against all odds, through his exceptional intelligence, diligence and hard work.

The narrative also deals with the context in which he lived and worked. It was the time of history when Christian missionaries made efforts to uplift the tribals through their spiritual, educational and health services. In her well-researched Introduction, Ivy Hansdak also mentions their contributions to the linguistic and ethnographic study of the Santals. In this work, these wide-ranging contributions are acknowledged with adequate evidence and support from the perspective of a Santal.

Furthermore, Ivy Hansdak contests the notion that the missionaries imposed their faith on the Santals. She maintains that it was the Santals who actively sought a new faith for its spiritual and temporal benefits. She cites the example of her great-grandfather who sought help from foreign missionaries to save his wife from the local villagers, who had declared her a witch and wanted to kill her. This sensitizes us to reexamine the connection between social transformation and religious conversion, from the tribal point of view. Many reformist agencies have been working amongst the Indian tribes for their uplift, but they have hardly bothered to learn what the tribal people themselves want. It is important to understand the tribal point of view, since it could be unique.

In an International Conference organized by Professor G. N. Devy in January 2008 at New Delhi, there was a debate in one of the sessions on whether the Christian tribes deserved to be called "tribes" and whether they retained all their indigenous cultural practices. A Bodo scholar had refuted the "either-or" view and opined that a tribal could be a Christian and still be a tribal. He had claimed that though he himself followed the Christian faith, he also practiced the rites and rituals of his community.

The same evidence is found in the life of Dr. Stephen Hansdak, who blended his faith with his cultural practices. He was rooted in his own culture and served his community while being a devout Christian. He lived and worked in a rural hospital in the Santal Parganas region, among his tribal brothers and sisters. Yet, while adopting the Santal way of life, he also had a strong bond with Christ. In the First Speech, he said: "...I learnt to trust God and accepted Jesus Christ as my personal Saviour and Master." He was also content with the simple life at Mohulpahari. Hence, he concluded the First Speech with these words: "Although it was difficult to work all my life in a rural hospital, I have found it very satisfying. Financially, there was not much gain, but mentally and spiritually, there has been job satisfaction and God's blessing...Now I can say that everything works out for good for them that love God."

The blend of spirituality, service and rootedness makes this narrative a different kind of autobiography. It is different from the Dalit autobiography that Sharankumar Limbale and Raj Kumar have written about. There is no trace of resistance here. Dr. Stephen Hansdak placed Christ at the centre of his life and served people since he believed that they were God's children. His life as a doctor combined faith and professionalism. So there was no scope for resistance. Had a Dalit Christian doctor of Dr. Stephen Hansdak's time written such a narrative, perhaps it might have had a similar tone and similar concerns.

It is striking to note the kind of hardship that Dr. Stephen Hansdak's family went through at a time of famine and scarcity. They had to survive on rice-gruel and jackfruits! While studying in a mission boarding school, his father used to pay the boarding fees in the form of vegetables that were grown on their field. This is a scene found in many remote tribal areas of India even today. Poor tribal parents put their children into boarding schools in spite of their poverty, and strive hard to educate them. When unable to pay the boarding fees in cash, they often bring bags full of rice grains, pulses or vegetables worth the same amount. Some of them walk over fifty kilometers with these bags on their shoulders, sweating and exhausted. They do this in the hope of giving their children a good education and better prospects for the future. This narrative calls to mind the same scene. Dr. Stephen Hansdak's intelligence and perseverance show that if the neglected are given opportunities, they can do wonders in life. Such talents should be nourished and encouraged.

The two speeches are well structured. Whereas the First Speech talks about Dr. Stephen Hansdak's life, the Second Speech is about his work and experience as a doctor. The chronology of his life and the other materials added remind one of Verrier Elwin's anthropological work, *Leaves from the Jungle: Life in a Gond Village*. Ivy Hansdak has meticulously collected materials, documented minute details and appended them to the speeches for the benefit of the reader. The Explanatory Notes and Bibliography will also help scholars to undertake further research in this area. The narrative will provide delightful reading for the general public. It is, moreover, my firm belief that it should be recommended particularly for the tribal youth because it will inspire them.

Anand Mahanand

EFL University, Hyderabad, India

A Glossary of Santali Terms

Chando	The sun and the moon; a month
Diku	A Hindu or Bengali of the better class; not applied to low caste Hindus or to Mohammedans
Handi	A rice-beer very popular with the Santals
Hapram	A collection of old men; also a congregational worker or elder
Hor hopon	Children of men; a human being; a Santal
Hul	The Santal Insurrection of 1855-56 against moneylenders
Jaher	The sacred grove with *saal* trees where Santals traditionally worship

Manjhi	The headman of a Santal village
Maran Buru	The principal spirit of the Santals; also called *Lita* sometimes
Mukhtar	A law agent or a petition writer
Ojha	A medicine man and a witch-finder
Pargana	A chief overlord above several village headmen; a division of a district or estate
Sarjom	The *saal* tree; its botanical name is *shorea robusta*
Tumda- tamak	Two kettle-drums made of iron, covered with the hide of a bullock or buffalo

List of Abbreviations

ACGME	Accreditation Council for Graduate Medical Education
AIDS	Acquired Immunodeficiency Syndrome
ANM	Auxiliary Nurse Midwife
CMAI	Christian Medical Association of India
CMC	Christian Medical College
CMS	Church Missionary Society
CNI	Church of North India
ECFMG	Educational Commission for Foreign Medical Graduates
EELC	Ebenezer Evangelical Lutheran Church
HIV	Human Immunodeficiency Virus

IHM	Indian Home Mission to the Santals
JMM	Jharkhand Mukti Morcha
LMP	Licensed Medical Practitioner
NELC	Northern Evangelical Lutheran Church
SMNC	Santal Mission of the Northern Churches
STD	Sexually Transmitted Disease

Dr. S. B. Hansdak after passing MBBS from CMC, Vellore, 1960

Citation for the Paul Harrison Award, 1988

Doctor Stephen Hansdak was a student of the Christian Medical College for his undergraduate and postgraduate medical training. By his unswerving fidelity to its motto, he has remained a true son and heir of his alma mater.

Stephen was born in a tribal community in the Santal Parganas which he first served as a village school teacher. After graduation from Vellore in 1961, he returned there to work in the hospital of the Northern Evangelical Lutheran Church in the village of Mohulpahari in the district of Dumka in Bihar. Because of the incessant need for surgical services in his isolated hospital, Hansdak returned to CMC for training towards the degree of Master of Surgery which he received in 1968.

For about a quarter of a century, Dr. Hansdak has served in Mohulpahari as a truly multicompetent physician the first and last resource for medical care in this isolated area. Under his able leadership, the bed strength of this small hospital grew to 130 and a school of nursing was added. Community Health services now reach out from Mohulpahari to a population of about 10,000. For many years, Dr. Hansdak has been the moving spirit behind the activities of both the Christian Medical Association and the Voluntary Health Association in the state of Bihar.

From his student days, Hansdak's life has been a demonstration of the enriching power of Christian discipleship. An active member of his church, he has served for long on its Synod and as the convener of its Medical Committee.

In recognition of a lifetime of faithful, devoted and effective service in the spirit of Christ to his own needy people in a remote rural part of our country, the Paul Harrison Award of 1988 is presented to Dr. Stephen Hansdak.

Christian Medical College
Vellore

10th October 1988.

MBBS Batch of 1955, CMC, Vellore

Dr. S.B. Hansdak with family at Vellore, 1967

Dr. and Mrs. Hansdak at Mohulpahari Christian Hospital, 1995

Introduction

In the expanding literature on Indian Adivasis, we do not meet many of those who, at quite an early date, were able to get an education. Even rarer, perhaps, are stories of those who, while benefiting from education, chose to stay in the 'tribal' areas and work among their own people. The present book, *A Doctor among the Santals: The Autobiography of Dr. Stephen B. Hansdak*, is presented to us by his scholar daughter, Ivy Imogene Hansdak. In the Editor's Introduction, she tells us about the context in time and space in which Dr. Stephen Hansdak lived and worked. The book represents an insider's perspective since Ivy Hansdak has interviewed her surviving kin in order to collect their childhood memories and reconstruct the family's history. In so doing, she has produced a narrative which not only concerns her own family story but provides a glimpse of the social history of the Santals during the late nineteenth and early twentieth centuries. The narrative also offers us a testimony of how the Scandinavian missionaries had succeeded in creating a Christian community around Dumka, not least because many Santals themselves took up the evangelizing task. In the beginning, these missionaries concentrated on the very basics of education, and their whole ideology, as well as their own background, was opposed to any idea of creating an intellectual elite. But Christian education developed considerably between 1905 and 1920, gradually offering an opportunity for social mobility.

The family story starts at the time where the missionaries were trying to build a Santal church by converting the chiefs. The conversion of Dr. Hansdak's grandfather, Palu Hansdak, to Christianity took place around 1880. The Great Bengal Famine of 1874 had affected many districts of the Santal Parganas region. In Nankar district, which included Benagaria, one of the mission's founders, Rev. H.P. Boerresen, was given charge of famine relief work by the colonial government. It was a time where the missionaries had already succeeded in strengthening the congregations around Dumka. In 1874, there were two thousands converts and each of the congregations had its Santal elders in charge of maintaining moral standards and a puritanical ethos.

The story of Palu Hansdak's conversion is particularly interesting, since Palu's young wife had been accused of witchcraft by an *ojha*, an accusation which could provoke the wrath of their neighbors since witches were often banned from the village and sometimes stoned to death.

The couple escaped from their village and took shelter in the Lutheran Mission in Ranga, where they converted to Christianity. In the early 1880s, the Scandinavian Mission was as remarkable for the small number of foreign missionaries as for the level of evangelizing activity among the converts. Like many others, Palu started to preach in order to convert other Santals. He also worked as a petition-writer. Finally, he was ordained pastor of Dumaria congregation in 1923, and was occupying this position when a small church was built there in 1932. While this story parallels other cases of conversion, it is interesting to note that it conforms to the model where a convert becomes a preacher and even a pastor, since the Santal Mission of the Northern Churches, in its early days, tried to maintain that "the Santals should be converted by Santals".

Information on the Mission's medical activities is useful, since Skrefsrud and Boerresen were at first not really concerned by having a doctor working for the mission. This was largely due to their Pietist attitude: life, death and health were in the hands of God, and the fate of people was determined by His will; those who had faith would be saved and gain salvation. Thus, it was relatively late that the Mission recruited a Danish doctor, Dr Johansen, who came with his wife to work at Benagaria in 1902. Nevertheless, there was high mortality, especially among children at the Mission, and it was only after a female doctor named Christine Larsen, who married Rev. P.O. Bodding, started to work in Mohulpahari that the situation started to improve.

Stephen Hansdak, born in 1931, was the son of Palu's eldest son. He studied in the local school until 1943. There was a time when he had to give up school for a year, due to his family's struggles against poverty. In 1944, he joined the Santal High School in Kaerabani, where he was a boarder in the boy's hostel. Here, he washed the plates and clothes of his classmates, since his parents had seven children and could not afford to buy soap for him. He was encouraged by different teachers, though he admits in his speeches that he had to overcome many difficulties. Yet, with a scholarship from the Mission, he was able to continue his higher studies in Ranchi and became a science teacher in the Kaerabani High School until 1955. The choice of science with biology was important, since this would enable him to enter a medical college later. Through assistance from the Mission - now the Church - he got a seat at the Christian Medical College in Vellore and could realize his dream of becoming a doctor. But, as he tells us, Vellore felt very far from home – he had never travelled in a train before – and he felt shy about his background and his bad English. He succeeded, however, and so was recruited by the Church as a junior doctor in the Mohulpahari Christian Hospital. In 1960, Stephen Hansdak married Alice Murmu, a Santal nurse. They were to form a couple of medical practitioners dedicated to rural medical service. Alice later became the Principal of the Church's training school for nurses while Stephen became the Medical Superintendent of the mission hospital.

The two speeches Dr Stephen Hansdak gave at a meeting of the CMC Vellore Alumni Association, USA Chapter, at Split Rock Resort, Philadelphia, must have been carefully prepared. We can see how Dr. Hansdak had selected his material to illustrate a few central themes. While the first speech relates to his life, the second speech relates to his career as a doctor. The theme of poverty - which emerges clearly in the first speech - is of special interest since it opens perspectives for further research on the period, especially during the war until Independence. His daughter mentions the difficulties he had to overcome especially in time of war and famine, when his family lived precariously on rice-gruel and jackfruit for weeks. She also tells us about one of her uncles, who joined the British army and returned in time to help the family financially. Interestingly, the uncle could not have had much trust in the 'law and order' of the period, since he had sewn his banknotes to the inside of his shirt, for safety.

The speeches of Dr Hansdak certainly have an oral quality, and the reader will note how strongly he insists on being able to keep a Santal identity. In the first speech, he stresses that like all Santal people - who were hunters and cultivators - he had the hunter's 'blood' in him. In Mohulpahari, he often went hunting and fishing. His story about how he shot his first leopard is full of life, as is the story of the big fish that pulled him into the water. We understand that the 'senior doctor' had responsibilities that went beyond the medical. But there was also the problem of being the 'universal doctor' since specialists were not available. He had no specialist training in gynecology yet when the second of the twins he was about to extract was lying athwart, he had to rely on his courses at medical college. We feel how relieved he was when all turned out well. He tells us about the problems of making a hospital work with insufficient resources in a backward area – and we understand that this is a situation which got no better when the Missions had to withdraw and the Church became independent. Several of the Mission's hospitals have had to close… and this was certainly not because the medical staff was too expensive. To finance a proper education for his children, he had to grow rice on paddy fields that he leased and work in his vegetable plot after hours, to earn a bit on the side.

We also understand how the doctor remains something of a magician – a modernized *ojha* – in the eyes of the people. He notes with relief that they do not hold the doctor responsible when the patient dies – "there was no consumer's society in those days" – and we realize that in the straitened circumstances, he must have been well aware that he could not work miracles. Here, his religion shows strongly: he feels that whatever he does is due to God's will. We get a picture of a man of courage and commitment who never hesitates to do his best in a difficult situation. Here, certainly, is an example of a member of the 'tribal elite' who did not forget his brethren but chose to remain and work among them.

The reader may feel dissatisfied with what he can learn through this book; certainly, we would have liked to know more. But we still know so little about the realities of the emergence of a tribal elite in India between the wars and in the early years of independence. Let us hope that others, like Ivy Hansdak, will dig into family memory and documents to give us more fragments of the history of these subaltern groups of India.

Marine Carrin and Harald Tambs-Lyche

Toulouse, France

Editor's Introduction

I

This book was conceived in a rather unusual manner. It began in May 1998, when my parents were invited as special guests to a meeting of the CMC Vellore Alumni Association, USA Chapter, at Split Rock Resort, Philadelphia, USA. There my father met many of his former classmates from CMC, Vellore, and delivered two speeches wherein he narrated the story of his early life in a Santal village, his struggles to become a doctor, and his career as a general surgeon at a rural mission hospital. This hospital was the Mohulpahari Christian Hospital, Santal Parganas, Bihar, India (now Dumka, Santhal Parganas, Jharkhand, India).[1]

---

[1] The term "Santal" has been spelt in two ways here – "Santal" and "Santhal". The former spelling was earlier used by all missionaries and other writers in their works while the latter spelling became standardized for administrative purposes after 1947.

My father died at the same hospital on 8 January, 2002, and was buried in a corner of its front lawns. A few months later, my mother showed me some faded pages that contained his two speeches delivered at the CMC Vellore Alumni Association meeting in 1998. In going through them, I realized that they preserved my father's 'autobiography'. It was not a lengthy one since the entire material covered less than ten typed sheets; yet the story within those few pages absorbed me.

As a *document of social history*, the narrative brought the reader in touch with the peripheral world of missionaries and tribal converts who lived in the Santal Parganas during the late nineteenth and early twentieth centuries. As an *autobiographical narrative*, it traced the narrator's long journey from a small Santal village, through his growing years, to a premier medical college, and finally to his life as a general surgeon in a primitive tribal area of eastern India. The narrator's own tribal background and familiarity with the customs of that area added to its authenticity. Written in simple English, it had the limpid quality of an oral tale told with humour and detachment. It revealed not only his phenomenal intelligence and service, but also his deep and personal faith in Christ. These qualities had formed the core of his character and made him one of the most revered men of Santal Parganas in his lifetime.

My decision to get my father's autobiographical narrative published was guided by two main considerations: firstly, it offered a rare glimpse into a different social world and secondly, it contained an alternative view of religious conversion among the indigenous/ adivasi/ tribal people of India. To begin with the first, the narrative spoke of a world that has long disappeared, a world where the primitive Santals first came in contact with modernity and cultural change. This occurred through many agencies but Christianity and Western education were the most prominent among them. My father was a beneficiary of both. He was the grandson of a Santal man named Palu Hansdak who converted to Christianity and became a pastor in the Santal Mission of the Northern Churches (later known as the Northern Evangelical Lutheran Church or NELC).[2]

As a child, I had often heard my parents speak of their past experiences but had never bothered to listen seriously. Then came a time when I started reading about my tribal identity. It began with an M.Phil course under Prof. Meenakshi Mukherjee at Jawaharlal Nehru University, New Delhi, which led to an M.Phil. dissertation on the

---

[2] The Santal Mission began as the Indian Home Mission to the Santals (IHM). It was renamed as the Santal Mission of the Northern Churches (SMNC) in 1910. In 1950, the name was changed to Ebenezer Evangelical Lutheran Church (EELC). Finally, in 1958, it was again renamed as the Northern Evangelical Lutheran Church (NELC).

topic "The Tribal as the 'Primitive' Other in Indian Literature". Here, I ventured into an interdisciplinary area that linked Indian literature with colonial anthropology. During the following years, the desire to know and understand my Santal Christian background grew stronger. I started reading all the books on Santal Mission history that I could find, but the material was very thin.[3] I then corresponded with some retired missionaries but learned that most of the books and documents were written in the Norwegian language and available only at the National Library, Oslo. Not surprisingly, my interest in the area started fading.

It was at this point that my father died and his speeches fell into my hands. All of a sudden, my imagination was fired again. But the going was still tough. To begin with,

---

[3] The most informative book in English available at that time was Olav Hodne's *The Seed Bore Fruit: A Short History of the Santal Mission of the Northern Churches, 1867-1967* (Calcutta: C.D. Media, 1967) but it was not a very detailed one. I knew of the existence of a more comprehensive history by Johan Nyhagen, *Santalmisjonens Historie I & II* (Oslo: Santalmisjonens Forlag, 1975), but this was in the Norwegian language and not accessible to me. It was only after the publication of Marine Carrin and Harald Tambs-Lyche's book, *An Encounter of Peripheries: Santals, Missionaries, and their Changing Worlds, 1867-1900* (New Delhi: Manohar, 2008), that I could finally gain some access to Nyhagen's work, since they had used it extensively in their research. I also gained access to another valuable book by Olav Hodne, *L.O. Skrefsrud: Missionary and Social Reformer among the Santals of Santal Parganas: With special reference to the period between 1867 and 1881* (Oslo: Forlaget Land Og Kirke, 1966).

I realized that my father's short narrative needed to be augmented with more material. The question was: what kind of material? I finally came up with a very simple solution – I decided to include a lengthy Introduction along with the speeches. This would not only provide a much-needed background to my father's life but also facilitate research by interested scholars.

I now come to the second reason for publishing these speeches. In the past few decades, tribal Christians in India have been subjected to various forms of denigration by mainstream Indian society. In most cases, their acceptance of a foreign religion has been treated contemptuously and dismissed as 'proselytisation'. This terminology has constructed them as passive and naïve subjects of conniving foreign missionaries. In the absence of any autobiographical narratives by tribal Christians, this perception has gained currency within mainstream Indian society. In recent times, it has been projected by militant Hindutva groups to justify the use of violence against tribal Christians and foreign missionaries.

My father's narrative directly contradicts this perception. In it, conversion is actively sought by the Santals both for its spiritual and temporal benefits. So when my father's grandmother was accused of witchcraft and threatened with death, she and her husband (my father's grandfather) turned to the mission for help. Their conversion followed and they slowly cleaved to the new faith. My great-grandfather, Palu Hansdak, went on to become a pastor and laid the foundation of an extended family, whose members have remained faithful Christians to this day.

Of late, I have also realized that it is necessary to re-examine the socio-cultural changes introduced by foreign missionaries among primitive tribal groups in colonial India. So this Introduction goes beyond Palu Hansdak's conversion to attempt a holistic view of the Santal Christian community. Marine Carrin and Harald Tambs-Lyche's recent work, *An Encounter of Peripheries: Santals, Missionaries and their Changing Worlds, 1867 – 1900*, has opened up new perspectives that will undoubtedly change the way Santal Christians are viewed by research scholars. It is hoped that this short autobiographical narrative from an insider's perspective will contribute to future research in this area.

II

My father's autobiographical narrative begins with his grandfather's story, probably in the 1880s. The story is set in the Santal Parganas region of eastern India, which was then part of the British-ruled Bengal Province. The background for the story, however, was laid much earlier. It may be traced back to the mid-nineteenth century when European missionaries first arrived in the Santal Parganas. The Baptists were the first to work among the Santals. They were followed by two Lutheran missionaries from Scandinavia named Rev. Lars Olsen Skrefsrud and Rev. Hans Peter Boerresen, who are today considered the real pioneers of mission work in the Santal Parganas. Skrefsrud, a Norwegian, and Boerresen, a Dane, had arrived in India in the early 1860s as missionary candidates to the Gossner Mission of Germany, then working among the Oraon tribe of Chotanagpur. There they met a Baptist missionary named Rev. E.C. Johnson, who told them about the Santal tribe of the Santal Parganas. Since their relations with the Gossner Mission had soured by then, the two Scandinavians decided to work among the Santals. In September 1867, a mission station named Ebenezer was founded by Skrefsrud, Boerresen and Johnson at Benagaria, in Nankar district, Santal Parganas. The mission that came into existence was called the Indian Home Mission to the Santals (IMH) or simply the Santal Mission.[4] Later, this Mission was solely managed by Skrefsrud and Boerresen.

Skrefsrud's life as a missionary and social reformer among the Santals has acquired a legendary quality over the years. He has been the subject of many hagiographic writings - biographical as well as imaginative - by Scandinavian writers. Commenting on this quality, Marine Carrin and Harald Tambs-Lyche write:

---

[4] Hodne, *The Seed Bore Fruit*, 11-12. Also Hodne, *L.O. Skrefsrud*, 71-72.

Missionary careers lend themselves to emplotment into hagiographical texts: their lives become legendary; the subjects themselves were clearly aware of this. Skrefsrud, for one, was one who succeeded in tailoring his activity to suit the myth. But as we get to know other characters, he becomes less exceptional than we may think. In the late nineteenth century adventure was eminently possible and sometimes, perhaps, unavoidable.[5]

Skrefsrud was born on 4 February, 1840, on a small tenant farm near Lillehammer, eastern Norway. His father, Ole Neilsen Skrefsrud, belonged to the artisan-husmann class while his mother, Eli Dosen, came from a gifted and influential family. As a boy, Skrefsrud had been greatly attached to her while despising his alcoholic father. Since he did not receive any formal education, his exceptional abilities were not known during these early years. As a youth, he was apprenticed to a coppersmith at Lillehammer and trained as a mechanic. Soon after, he started drinking and fell into bad company. In 1858, at the age of eighteen years, he went on a drinking binge with some friends and broke into a shop. He was arrested and sentenced to prison for four years but was released after serving a sentence of two years and four months.

In prison, Skrefsrud went through an intense spiritual experience, during which he had a vision of Christ and decided on his future calling as a missionary. Thereafter, his exceptional intellectual gifts became apparent. He read

---

⁵ Carrin and Tambs-Lyche, *An Encounter of Peripheries*, 12.

philosophers like Novalis, Kierkegaard, Swedenborg and some conventional religious authors. He also taught himself German, English and Latin, besides some French and Greek.[6] When the seamstress to whom he was affianced refused to become a missionary's wife, he married Anne Onsum, who had visited him in prison. Skrefsrud's biographer, Olav Hodne, sheds light on the emotional struggles that Skrefsrud went through during this time, pointing out that Anne Onsum never replaced his first love. Hodne quotes these words written by Skrefsrud in a letter to his friend and confidante, Rev. Ludvig Hertel, in 1877:

> I had to give up a many years' fiancée in order to follow the Lord's calling; and if any man at any time has loved deeply, then it was I. It was as if soul and body should be pulled apart, but then the Lord helped me to do it with joy.[7]

On leaving prison, Skrefsrud applied at a seminary run by the Norwegian Missionary Society in Stavanger but was rejected as an ex-convict. Then an acquaintance urged him to go to Berlin and meet Hans Peter Boerresen, a Dane, who had helped many Norwegian students. So, in 1862, Skrefsrud arrived at Berlin. There he met the Boerresens, who would become his life-long friends and coworkers in India.

---

[6] *Ibid.*, 55.

[7] Hodne, *L. O. Skrefsrud*, 52-53.

Hans Peter Boerresen was born at Copenhagen, Denmark, in 1825 and grew up there. Like Skrefsrud, he had also trained to become a mechanic. In 1852, he immigrated to Berlin, where his married sister used to live, and soon started working as a master mechanic. A year later, he had a spiritual experience and grew interested in mission work. Thereafter, he met and became friends with J.F.C. Hempel, an Evangelical from Brandenburg. Two years later, Boerresen married Hempel's daughter, Caroline.[8]

On the advice of the Boerresens, Skrefsrud entered the Gossnerian Mission School at Berlin and completed the exams within a year. The two men were then urged to join the Gossner Mission Society as missionary candidates, to which they agreed. In 1863, Skrefsrud arrived with the Boerresens in India. Two years later, Skrefsrud's fiancée, Anne Onsum, joined him in India and they were married at Purulia, on 23 May 1865.[9]

After the establishment of the Ebenezer mission station at Benagaria, the Indian Home Mission (IHM) developed gradually under the combined influence of the Lutherans

---

[8] Carrin and Tambs-Lyche, Op. cit., 56-57.

[9] Though Carrin and Tambs-Lyche write that Skrefsrud married Anne Onsum before his departure to India, Hodne states that the marriage took place after his arrival in India. Hodne cites both Skrefsrud's *Autobiography* of 1892 and Anne Onsum's letters. Carrin and Tambs-Lyche, *Op.* cit., 57 and Hodne, *L. O. Skrefsrud*, 52.

and the Baptists. By 1880, however, the IHM had broken away from Baptist influence and established closer ties with the Anglican and Presbyterian circles of England and Scotland.[10] As for Skrefsrud and Boerresen, they proved to be a well-matched team. Besides evangelising among the Santals, Boerresen went on several fund-raising tours among various denominational circles while Skrefsrud busied himself with linguistic and ethnographic research. As mentioned earlier, Skrefsrud had a phenomenal gift for languages. Hence, he soon involved himself with various projects such as writing books on Santal customs and traditions, on Santali grammar, and translating the New Testament into Santali.

Like other tribal/indigenous languages of India, Santali was originally an oral language without a script. The first book on the Santali language, *An Introduction to the Santal Language*, had used the Bengali alphabet for Santali words. Written by a Baptist missionary named Rev. J. Phillips and published in 1852, it contained a Santali grammar as well as a simple Santali vocabulary.[11] Later writers, however, discarded the use of the Bengali script. Instead, the Latin

---

[10] Hodne, *Ibid.*, 71-72. According to Hodne, Skrefsrud even received second baptism in the Baptist Mission Society, thereby becoming a professed Baptist for some time. This phase did not last long and the two pioneers reverted back to Lutheranism.

[11] *Ibid.*, 218-219.

or Roman alphabet was standardized with the inclusion of diacritical marks and generally accepted by all missionaries working among the Santals. Skrefsrud also used the Roman script in all his writings.

Skrefsrud proved to be a prolific writer. Besides translating the New Testament into Santali, he also collected ethnographic data that became a veritable storehouse of information for future anthropologists and scholars. He documented Santal customs and traditions in a Santali book, *Horkoren Mare Hapramko Reak' Katha*,[12] wrote a grammar book in Santali and started collecting material for a Santali dictionary. But perhaps his most enduring work, especially for the music-loving Santals, was a hymnology which used traditional Santali tunes in church hymns. Of this, a later missionary named Rev. Johannes Gausdal said:

> ."...the Christianizing of a number of the melodies in common use among the Santals, is one of the most remarkable features in the Santal hymnology...there can be no doubt that the Santal Church will come to look upon Skrefsrud as the rarely gifted man who discovered a golden chord in the

---

[12] This valuable book was a *verbatim* recording of the words of a Santal guru called Kolean Haram by L.O. Skrefsrud. It was originally published in Santali in 1887, then translated into English by P.O. Bodding and published as *Traditions and Institutions of the Santals* in 1942. A reprinted and edited publication appeared in India in 1994. Ref. P.O. Bodding, L.O. Skrefsrud and Sten Konow, *Traditions and Institutions of the Santals: Horkoren Mare Hapramko Reak' Katha* (New Delhi: Bahumukhi Prakashan, 1994).

soul of the Santal people, and played it to their joy and admiration, thereby drawing them to the eternal God."[13]

Like many other missionaries working among depressed groups, Skrefsrud was also drawn into social reform. After the Santal *Hul* or Insurrection of 1855-56, many Santals had lost their land and there was general unrest among them. Skrefsrud soon became their spokesman. He met Sir George Campbell, the Lieutenant Governor of Bengal Province, along with a group of Santal chiefs and presented the cause of the people. Under his influence, a new law called the "Regulation for the peace and good governance of the territory known as the Sonthal Pergunnahs" was issued by the Bengal Government on 1 May, 1872. Commenting on this, Olav Hodne writes:

> "The Regulation, the Magna Charta of the Santals, gave the Lieutenant Governor full power to appoint officers to make a settlement of landed rights, to restore dispossessed manjhis and others, to settle rents, and to record customs and practices of the people.
>
> It also introduced a usury law limiting the accumulation of interest on debts, and it determined what laws were to be in force in the Santal Parganas. The principals laid down in the Regulation of 1872 have been the guiding principles in the administration of the Santals of the Santal Parganas up to the present day."[14]

---

[13] Cited by Hodne, *L.O. Skrefsrud,* 232, from Johannes Gausdal, *Contributions to Santal Hymnology* (Bergen: 1935), 21-23.

[14] Hodne, *Ibid.,* 252.

During the following years, as more converts were won, many more mission stations were built. Some of these were at Dumka, Mohulpahari, Basetkundi, Haripur, Maharo, Kaerabani, Simaldohi, Majdiha and Karikador, among others. Ironically, opposition to the Christian missionaries also appeared during these years. This was probably triggered by the missionaries' inflexible attitude to certain Santal customs and habits that were perceived as detrimental to Christian morality. They particularly frowned upon the Santals' fondness for a kind of rice-beer called *handi*, their popular communal folk-dances and their use of two popular drums called *tumda* and *tamak*, which were an integral part of Santal festivities as well as rebellions.

During these years, a rather puritanical strain of Christianity was imposed upon the converts of the Santal Mission. The consumption of *handi* was strictly forbidden, as also participation in the communal folk-dances; moreover, while the singing of folk-songs was permitted and even encouraged, the use of the *tumda* and *tamak* was also forbidden. This puritanism has persisted among many Santal Christians of the NELC even today, though attempts are also being made by the younger generation to reintroduce some of their customs and practices. In retrospect, it might be claimed that Skrefsrud's own bitter experience of alcoholism as a youth in Norway led him to impose this regimen of austerity upon the exuberant and pleasure-loving Santals. Interestingly, a similar austerity is found among many missionaries who worked in Asia and Africa. In many such cases, not only were drinking and dancing banned for converts but attempts were also made to clothe the native women. Hence, Skrefsrud was not exceptional in this regard.

The opposition to missionaries first surfaced in 1872, when a Santal chieftain called Matru Pargana and his brother, Naran Manjhi, the headman of Benagaria village, called a council of all *manjhis* in order to drive away the missionaries. But before this council could meet, Matru Pargana was arrested by the District Magistrate for some past offence and jailed. He was released from jail eight months later, broken in health. After vainly seeking help from many medicine-men, Matru Pargana was finally cured by Skrefsrud. Thereafter, his attitude to Christianity changed and he was baptized soon after.[15] Matru Pargana's conversion saw the beginning of a new phase of evangelisation in the Santal Parganas.

At this point, it is necessary to examine some pertinent issues raised by Matru Pargana's remarkable story. Matru Pargana's arrest and imprisonment at a very crucial juncture by the British colonial administration effectively turned the tide in favour of the Scandinavian missionaries. It is impossible to ascertain whether Matru Pargana's arrest was

---

[15] Hodne, *Ibid.*, 166- 167. Also Carrin and Tambs-Lyche, *op.cit.*, 124-125.

carried out with the sole purpose of defusing a volatile situation or whether it was also intended to assist the missionaries in their evangelising efforts. But his release and subsequent conversion to Christianity occurred in circumstances that certainly shed dubious light on the parties concerned, particularly when the unequal power dynamics of the colonial period is taken into consideration.

Soon after, another controversy regarding the Santal Mission surfaced. The Great Bengal Famine of 1874 had affected many districts of the Santal Parganas region. In Nankar district, which included Benagaria, Boerresen was given charge of famine relief work by the colonial government. Skrefsrud then being on a visit to Europe, Boerresen used this opportunity to preach the Gospel and win new converts. This was strongly criticized in a newspaper article by a prominent Baptist missionary named Rev G. Kerry.[16] Interestingly, it has been stated by Olav Hodne that many of the new converts continued to remain within the fold even after the famine ended, contrary to expectations. He further reports that, at the end of 1874, the Santal Mission numbered about two thousand adults and about four thousand children, a majority of them living in Nankar district.[17]

---

[16] Hodne, *Ibid.*, 169-172. Also Carrin and Tambs-Lyche, *Ibid.*, 130-131.

[17] Hodne, *Ibid.*, 175.

The mass movement towards Christianity did not last long, especially after the spread of the Kherwar movement in the mid-1870s. This was led by a Santal leader named Bhagrit, who was enthroned as a Raja. While the Kherwar movement purported to liberate the Santals from colonial rule and missionary influence, it also showed a clear trend towards Hinduisation, with its followers taking to vegetarianism, killing 'impure' animals such as pigs and fowls, venerating the cow and worshipping a new deity called Ram Chando - who combined the Hindu deity Ram with the Santali word "chando" that stands for both sun and moon.[18] But the mission work continued and more missionaries arrived to join the pioneers.

During these years, the booming tea industry of Assam and the growing land-hunger of the Santals caused Skrefsrud to try a bold experiment. He decided to purchase a large tract of land in Assam and settle a group of Santal converts there. Consequently, some thirty square miles of land was purchased in the Goalpara district of Assam and on 8 February, 1881, Boerresen arrived with the first group of settlers. This consisted of forty-two Santal families, who had came by the long route via Calcutta by train and up the Brahmaputra by steamer to Dhubri, then walked the last thirty miles from Dhubri to Goalpara. Boerresen alone rode on an elephant lent to him by the Assam Government.

---

[18] Hodne, *Ibid.*, 265-287. Also Carrin and Tambs-Lyche, Ibid., 204-214.

A week later, another group of thirteen families arrived. The settlement that came into existence was known as the Assam Santal Colony. In 1890, a tea plantation adjacent to the Colony was also purchased. This was called the Mornai Tea Estate.[19]

At the Assam Santal Colony, Skrefsrud tried to create a wholesome Christian environment. While the social institutions of the old country were preserved to a large extent, there were restrictions on certain matters. To sum up, no heathen worship or practices were allowed, no intoxicating liquor was brewed, sold or drunk, no dancing, and no Sunday labour, buying or selling were permitted. It was hoped that this Christian environment would 'develop' the Santal character and wean the converts away from their vices. Here, Skrefsrud seems to fit into the mould of the conventional missionary who wages war against alcoholism, promiscuity and heathenism. His uniqueness lies, as Marine Carrin and Harald Tambs-Lyche point out, in his view of the Santals "as a nation with a distinct culture to be respected..." This view, they further say, may be contrasted with the "negation" found in the view of many missionaries working among the tribes of southern Africa.[20]

---

[19] Hodne, *Ibid.*, 318-330. Also Carrin and Tambs-Lyche, Ibid., 251-260.

[20] Carrin and Tambs-Lyche, *Ibid.*, 13.

Boerresen died at Benagaria on 23 September, 1901. Skrefsrud lived on for nine more years but suffered a decline in health. One and a half years before his death, he signed a document appointing Paul Olav Bodding as the sole manager of the Santal Mission. He died at Benagaria on 11 December, 1910.[21]

P.O. Bodding went on to take over Skrefsrud's legacy in the field of linguistic and ethnographic research. Like Skrefsrud, he was a Norwegian with a rare gift for languages. After resigning from his administrative duties in 1923, he moved to Mohulpahari and busied himself with literary work. His main task was the translation of the Bible into Santali. While some parts of the Bible had already been translated and revised by earlier missionaries, the entire Bible was finally translated by him and published in Santali in 1929.[22] Bodding also added to Skrefsrud's hymnology by translating more than thirty Norwegian hymns into

---

[21] Both Skrefsrud and Boerresen were buried in a cemetery near Ebenezer Church, Benagaria.

[22] Bodding's version of the Bible was published at the Benagaria Mission Press in 1929. It is called the "Benagaria version" and is a direct translation from the Hebrew and Greek languages. The Anglicans have also translated the New Testament and parts of the Old Testament. This has been published by The Bible Society of India and is called the "Taljhari version". The Taljhari version is a translation from the Hindi and English languages, so the differences between the two versions are many. In 1962, a joint translation of the New Testament was published by The Bible Society of India. Elizabeth Doerdal, *Paul Olaf Bodding: His Call and his Service* (Dumka: Sharda Press, 2007), 10.

Santali. Some other notable works by him were *A Chapter of Santal Folklore* (1924), *Santal Folk Tales*, Part I-III (1925-29), *A Santali Grammar for Beginners* (1929), *Studies in Santal Medicine and Connected Folklore*, Part I, II & III (1925,1927 & 1940), *A Santal Dictionary*, I-V, (1929-36) and *Traditions and Institutions of the Santals* (1942: translation of Skrefsrud's *Horkoren Mare Hapramko reak'* *Katha* from Santali into English).

Among all his achievements, Bodding's work as a lexicographer is perhaps the most remarkable. He was the author of a monumental work, *A Santal Dictionary*, which was actually an encyclopedia-cum-dictionary in five volumes and took eight years to complete. Like Skrefsrud, Bodding had a group of Santal collaborators to help him. Skrefsrud had learnt Santali from an old man named Khudu. After Khudu's death, Biram Hansdak had become Skrefsrud's main collaborator. When Bodding took over the literary work from Skrefsrud, Biram naturally became his teacher and assistant. Bodding usually had about five Santal collaborators at Mohulpahari; of them, at least one would be illiterate. Besides Biram Hansdak, two other well-known collaborators of Bodding were Sagram Murmu, a schoolteacher with a great fluency in writing in his own language and Mongol, an illiterate leper with a rich knowledge of Santali. For Bodding, these men were the "living lexica".[23]

---

[23] Carrin and Tambs-Lyche, *op.cit.*, 324-327.

Bodding preferred the quiet solitude of Mohulpahari to the busy activity of Benagaria. He had arrived at Benagaria in January 1890, but had soon moved to Mohulpahari. It was at Mohulpahari that his first wife, Clara Braathen, was buried when she died soon after their marriage.[24] It was also here that his third wife, Dr. Christine Larsen, worked in a small hospital from 1923 to 1934. Bodding built a large and stately bungalow at Mohulpahari, where most of his literary work was done. In April 1934, the Boddings left India for the last time. They lived in Oslo, Norway, until the last volume of *A Santal Dictionary* was published in 1936. They then moved to Odense, Denmark, where P.O. Bodding died on 25 September, 1938.

Seventeen years after the Boddings left India, their spacious bungalow was converted into a general hospital and dedicated on 18 February, 1951. Called the Mohulpahari Christian Hospital, its first Medical Superintendent was an American missionary doctor from

---

[24] P.O. Bodding married Clara Braathen on 18 December, 1891. She died of pneumonia on 26 April 1892. Five years later, on 8 November, 1897, Bodding married Ingeborg Bahr, who was the widowed daughter of Rev. H.P. Boerresen and Caroline Boerresen. This marriage ended when she eloped with an unnamed Muslim in 1899. Bodding and Ingeborg Bahr were divorced in 1921; in 1923, he married Dr. Christine Larsen of Denmark and settled with her at Mohulpahari. Elizabeth Doerdal, Op. cit., pp. 16-17. A different version of Bodding's second marriage is found in Carrin and Tambs-Lyche, *Ibid.*, 299.

Minnesota, USA, named Dr. Kristofer Hagen.[25] It was here that my father worked for over thirty years of his life, and became its first Indian and Santal Medical Superintendent.

III

My father's autobiographical narrative begins with his grandfather, Palu Hansdak, who probably converted to Christianity sometime in the 1880s. At this point, the narrative is rather sketchy in nature but, with painstaking research, I have managed to reconstruct my great-grandfather's life. I began by interviewing my two surviving paternal aunts, Euniki and Salomi, and then collated their childhood memories with scraps of information gathered from miscellaneous sources.[26]

---

[25] Dr. Kristofer Hagen has left behind an interesting account of his experiences as a missionary doctor in India, South Vietnam, Ethiopia, Taiwan and Honduras in his book, *Third World Encounters: Dreams of Development* (Maple Grove, MN: Nystrom Publishing Company, 1984).

[26] My paternal aunts, Salomi and Euniki, are both younger than my father and were his only surviving siblings at the time of writing this book. Since the interviews were conducted in Santali and in conditions that were far from ideal, I decided to video-record them for future reference. My mother, Alice Hansdak, was also interviewed at the same time. I also interviewed a distant uncle, Hanuk Hansdak, who had studied with my father at Benagaria Boys' School. Besides these sources, I also used the *Panji 2008* (Yearbook 2008) of NELC, Dumka, the Santali newsletter, *Jugsirijol*, July 2001, and Olav Hodne's book, *The Seed Bore Fruit*, which contains a List of Pastors in an Appendix.

Palu Hansdak was born in the village of Bijaypur, in the Santal Parganas, in 1862.[27] Being an intelligent man with some education, he worked as a *mukhtar* or petition-writer. He was happily married, owned a small plot of land and had the simple needs of his class. Then a storm burst upon him that would change his life forever. His young wife was accused of witchcraft by the village *ojha* (witch-finder) and threatened with death. To escape the wrath of their neighbours, the young couple fled from Bijaypur at night and took shelter at a Lutheran mission in Ranga. This was called the Niyadih congregation and they were given shelter by the village *hapram* or preacher. Here, they converted to Christianity and Palu Hansdak started working both as a preacher and a petition-writer. In 1923, at the age of 61 years, he was ordained as the pastor of Dumaria congregation of the Santal Mission of the Northern Churches.[28] Since Dumaria was at some distance from Ranga, he was given a plot of land there by the *manjhi* to build his house. In 1932, when a small church was dedicated at Dumaria, Palu Hansdak was its pastor.[29]

---

[27] Olav Hodne, *The Seed Bore Fruit*, 196. Here, an Appendix contains a cryptic mention of my great-grandfather: "26. PALU HASDAK', Born in 1862. Ordained 7 October, 1923. Died 26 July, 1941."

[28] Now called the Northern Evangelical Lutheran Church (NELC).

[29] *Panji 2008* (Yearbook of the NELC, 2008), 27.

Palu Hansdak married three times. He fled Bijaypur with his first wife, to whom he was perhaps the most devoted. She gave birth to six children, four sons and two daughters. After her death, he married again but his second wife died childless (though they adopted a girl). Many years later, Palu Hansdak got married for the third time at the ripe age of seventy years. One child, a son, was born of this union. Palu Hansdak remained the pastor of Dumaria till his death on 26 July, 1941, at the age of seventy-nine years.

My father was the son of Palu Hansdak's eldest son, Kistu Hansdak and his wife, Roshni. There were ten children in Kistu Hansdak's family - six sons and four daughters – but two of the sons died in childhood. My father was born on 17 July, 1931.[30] He was the seventh child and the fifth son, with two sisters younger than him (an elder brother and a younger brother died). Kistu Hansdak worked as a teacher in a local primary school and also did some farming. My father's mother, Roshni, was reputed to be a woman of strong and dominating personality who ran her household with an iron hand. There still exist many family anecdotes about the stern discipline she imposed on her eight children. My father began his education at the local school, which had classes

---

[30] Dr. Hansdak's birth-date was later changed to 18 March, 1933. This is the birth-date on all his certificates, but he was actually born on 17 July, 1931.

only up to Class III. After completing Class III, his education was interrupted for one year because they ran short of money.

It was the year 1943 and the entire land was in the grips of a devastating famine. Further-a-field, World War II was raging and its repercussions were also felt in my grandfather's family. One of my father's elder brothers was removed from school and drafted as a peon in the British India army. This was a time of starvation and intense suffering for the people of the Santal Parganas. Some were reduced to eating leaves and the bark of trees. In my grandfather's house, the meager supply of rice started running short. Then a miracle saved them – a jackfruit tree in the front yard started bearing fruit! My grandfather's family lived precariously on rice-gruel and jackfruit for some weeks. This lean period finally ended with the return of my father's elder brother, Emmanuel, from the British India army in 1944. Fearing robbery on the journey home, he had sewn all his money to the inner side of his shirt!

After living at home for one year, my father was sent to the Kaerabani Santal High School in 1944. This was a boarding school for Santal boys run by missionaries at Kaerabani mission. Here, my father excelled in his studies and managed to catch the attention of the Principal, an American missionary named Rev. Harold Riber, who encouraged him to study medicine. Thus began my father's eventful journey into a new world of knowledge and opportunity. After passing the Annual Matriculation Examination of 1952 in the First Division, he went to Ranchi University to study Intermediate in Science (with Biology). He then worked for a year as a Science teacher at his old school in Kaerabani. In 1955, he applied for the MBBS course at Christian Medical College, Vellore, Tamil Nadu, but was rejected for his poor performance in spoken English. However, after Rev. Riber's personal intervention on his behalf, my father was accepted for admission in the MBBS course of 1955.[31]

The first year of MBBS at CMC, Vellore, must have been an extremely harrowing time for my father. He was far away from home, alone and friendless. Most of his classmates belonged to urban, middle-class society and were educated in English-medium schools. My father alone came from a remote, tribal society and a Hindi-medium school. But he had studied English as a compulsory subject at school and could read and write it tolerably well, though his speech was painfully slow. During this time, a burning desire to excel consumed him and drove him on. This lonely time came to an end when he scored top marks in Physiology in the First Final Examination. Thereafter, he

---

[31] My father was the third Santal student at CMC, Vellore. The other two were: Dr. Aloka Marandi of the CNI Church (MBBS Batch of 1951) and Dr. Baha Hembrom of the Methodist Church (MBBS Batch of 1952). However, my father was the first Santal doctor who passed the postgraduate MS course in General Surgery from CMC, Vellore, in 1968.

increased in confidence and found more friends among his classmates.

The next few years would lead him from one success to another. He graduated with the MBBS degree from CMC, Vellore, in 1960, and then did internship for one year. By then, he was also married to my mother, Alice Murmu, who had a degree in General Nursing from CMC, Ludhiana. In May 1961, he returned from Vellore and joined as a junior doctor at the Mohulpahari Christian Hospital. My mother joined as a staff nurse at Mohulpahari later that year.

This was my parents' first stint at Mohulpahari and it lasted from May 1961 to January 1965. By 1963, three children were born to them but they lost one in a drowning accident. Dr. Kristofer Hagen was the Medical Superintendent in 1961. There was also Dr. B.B. Chatterjee, a Bengali Hindu with an LMP (Licensed Medical Practitioner) degree. Two other doctors who became Medical Superintendents during this time were Dr. Egil Ofstad, from Norway, and Dr. William R. Scott, from the USA.

The going was very rough at times. Since mission service did not pay much, my parents soon had financial difficulties. This was compounded by the demands made by our extended family of relatives. My father was also thinking of higher studies by then. In 1963, he appeared for the ECFMG Examination and passed it.[32] This meant that he could immigrate to the United States with his family and practice there as a doctor. A bold, new ambition entered his mind and he was in the process of preparing for immigration when Dr. William R. Scott persuaded him to remain in India. But to satisfy his aspirations for higher studies, a scholarship was arranged so that he could apply for the MS course at CMC, Vellore.

In January 1965, my father returned to CMC, Vellore, and joined the MS course in General Surgery. My mother was then pregnant with their fourth child and she remained behind at Mohulpahari. I was born at Mohulpahari Christian Hospital in May 1965; it being a caesarean section delivery, Dr. B.B. Chatterjee operated on my mother while my father (then on leave) assisted him. Later, in December 1965, my mother came to Vellore along with the children. She worked as a staff nurse there till June 1967, and then applied for a 10-month PG course in Nursing Administration and Education at CMC, Vellore. My father passed his MS Exam in March 1968, while my mother got her PG degree a month later, in April 1968.

---

[32] The ECFMG or Educational Commission for Foreign Medical Graduates was and still is an examination for international medical graduates to enter residency or fellowship in the United States. It is accredited by the Accreditation Council for Graduate Medical Education (ACGME).

In May 1968, my parents returned to Mohulpahari Christian Hospital for the second time. Ms. Alice Axelson, who was then the Nursing School Principal, was the Acting Medical Superintendent. My father immediately joined as a doctor and was appointed the Medical Superintendent in December 1969. My mother also joined as a sister tutor at Mohulpahari Nursing School and was appointed the Nursing School Principal in December 1969. They would hold these posts for over twenty-five years, until my father's retirement in April 1998, to become a Senior Consultant at the Hospital.

The years from 1969 to 1998 would be occupied with hard and grueling labour, relieved by many moments of success and adventure. My father attended the International Congress of Christian Physicians thrice, at Singapore, Canada and Switzerland, in the years 1969, 1972 and 1978, respectively. Along with my mother, he travelled to the USA twice, in 1972 and 1998. Furthermore, they were invited to visit old friends in Norway and Denmark.

My father was also appointed the Regional Secretary of the Christian Medical Association of India (CMAI) for fifteen years and the President of the Bihar Voluntary Heath Association for three years. Within the NELC, he held several posts at different times; he was member of the Church Committee, the Church Synod and the

Diocesan Council. In 1998, he was the Chairman of the Constitution Revision Committee of NELC.

This success story continued on other fronts as well. During the 1970s, the Hospital became a training centre for fourth year medical students from the USA who qualified under the *Reader's Digest* International Fellowship program. Here, my father trained them in tropical medicine with rural patients. In the 1980s, a new Hospital Block was added to the old building and the bed-strength was increased.[33]

In 1988, my father was honoured with the Paul Harrison Award by CMC, Vellore. This honour is conferred on an alumnus of CMC, Vellore, for outstanding service in a rural area. The Citation of the Award read:

> *"For about a quarter of a century, Dr. Hansdak has served in Mohulpahari as a truly multicompetent physician, the first and last resource for medical care in this remote area...In recognition of a lifetime of faithful, devoted and effective service in the spirit of Christ to his own needy people in a remote rural part of our country, the Paul Harrison Award of 1988 is presented to Dr. Stephen Hansdak."*

A year later, in 1989, he made a brief foray into politics by contesting the Shikaripara Vidhan Sabha seat as a candidate

---

[33] This is mentioned in a letter written by Mrs. William R. Scott to Dr. Kristofer Hagen, and quoted by him in *Third World Encounters*, 206.

of the Congress Party. He lost to Nalin Soren of the Jharkhand Mukti Morcha (JMM) by a narrow margin. He remained, however, on excellent terms with all local political leaders across party lines.[34]

In March 2001, my father finally retired from Mohulpahari Christian Hospital to help my brother at his private clinic in Dumka. Less than a year later, he passed away due to cardiac failure on 8 January, 2002. The funeral service was attended by a large number of people, after which his body was buried at Mohulpahari Christian Hospital on 10 January, 2002. His grave carries this inscription:

> "And he shall be like a tree planted by the rivers of water, that bringeth forth his fruit in his season; his leaf also shall not wither; and whatsoever he doeth shall prosper."
>
> - Psalm 1:3, *Old Testament*

IV

As mentioned earlier, my father's simple narrative is both an autobiography and a document of social history. However, it stands apart from other Indian autobiographies for many reasons. It may be compared/ contrasted with the Dalit autobiography and the Indian Christian

---

[34] This was amply demonstrated by the fact that several political leaders, including Sibu Soren, Stephen Marandi and Nalin Soren of JMM, paid their respects to him after death.

autobiography but it would be found to be different from either because it occupies a unique discursive space of its own. In his recent work, *Dalit Personal Narratives*, Raj Kumar has pointed out that "…the very process of writing autobiography by the dalit is a form of resistance against various forms of oppression."[35] By contrast, speech/ writing in my father's autobiographical narrative is not used as a form of resistance.

Yet, my father belonged to the Santal community, which is an indigenous/ tribal/ adivasi community of eastern India and often clubbed together with dalit communities for administrative purposes. It is notable that the Indian tribes have hardly written any autobiographies, unlike the more politically-aware dalits. One of the few exceptions is C.K. Janu's autobiography, *Mother Forest*, though it originates as an oral narrative in Malayalam.[36] My father's autobiographical narrative may be said to contain an oral quality because it began as a speech. However, it was not spontaneous speech; rather, it was a carefully-prepared speech delivered in front of an immigrant audience at Philadelphia, USA. Hence, it actually combines the

---

[35] Raj Kumar, *Dalit Personal Narratives: Reading Caste, Nation and Identity* (New Delhi: Orient Blackswan, 2010), 150.

[36] C.K. Janu's autobiography was written down by Bhaskaran in Malayalam and then translated into English by N. Ravi Shankar. Ref. Bhaskaran, *Mother Forest: The Unfinished Story of C.K. Janu* (New Delhi: Kali for Women, 2004).

qualities of several narrative practices – both oral and written.

When compared with the Indian Christian autobiographies left behind by some upper caste converts like Nehemiah Goreh, Pandita Ramabai and Lakshmibai Tilak, my father's autobiography contains a conversion narrative with a difference. So while upper caste narratives emphasized the spiritual illumination that preceded their conversion, my father's narrative begins with Palu Hansdak's flight from witchcraft that preceded his conversion. Here, the temporal motivations of conversion gain prominence over the spiritual ones. Yet, the narrative goes on to construct an ideal Santal Christian world. The declaration of personal faith in Christ, made by my father in the first speech, also brings this narrative closer to the traditional Christian autobiography.

Ivy Imogene Hansdak

Jamia Millia Islamia, New Delhi, India

Chronology of
Dr. Stephen B. Hansdak's
Life (1931-2002)

1931	Born at Dumaria village, Santal Parganas (now in Deoghar district, Jharkhand) on 17 July, 1931
1943	Studied at the local primary school till Standard III and left it in 1943; had to stop his schooling for one year, from 1943 to 1944, due to poverty
1944	Joined Standard IV at the Kaerabani Santal High School, Dumka, in 1944; was a boarder in the Boys' Hostel
1952	Passed the Annual Matriculation Exam of 1952 in the First Division
1952-54	Studied Intermediate in Science (with Biology) at Ranchi College, Bihar, from 1952 to 1954
1954-55	Worked as a Science teacher at the Kaerabani Santal High School, Dumka, from 1954 to 1955

1955	Joined the MBBS course at CMC, Vellore, Tamil Nadu, in 1955
1960	Married Alice Murmu, who had a General Nursing degree from CMC, Ludhiana, in January 1960; Passed the MBBS Final Exam from CMC, Vellore (under Madras University) in 1960
1960-61	Did internship work at CMC, Vellore, for one year from 1960 to 1961; Alice did Midwifery training at St. Columbus Hospital, Hazaribagh, Bihar; first child, a daughter named Sylvia, was born on 28 March, 1961; joined as a junior doctor at Mohulpahari Christian Hospital, Dumka, in May 1961; Alice also joined as a staff nurse in November 1961
1962	Second child, a daughter named Eva, was born on 25 August, 1962
1963	Eldest daughter, Sylvia, died in a drowning accident on 2 February, 1963; passed the ECFMG Exam in 1963
1964	Third child, a son named Christopher, was born on 8 January, 1964
1965	Returned to CMC, Vellore, for MS degree in General Surgery, in January 1965; Alice remained at Mohulpahari; fourth child, a daughter named Ivy, was born on 26 May, 1965;

Alice arrived in Vellore with their three children in December 1965

1967   Alice joined a 10-month PG course in Nursing Administration and Education at CMC, Vellore, in 1967

1968   Passed the MS Exam from CMC, Vellore, in March 1968; Alice passed the PG course in Nursing Administration and Education in April 1968; returned to Mohulpahari Christian Hospital, Dumka, along with Alice and three children in May 1968

1969   Became the Medical Superintendent of Mohulpahari Christian Hospital in December 1969; Alice became the Principal of Mohulpahari Nursing School at the same time; attended the International Congress of Christian Physicians at Singapore in 1969, then visited Norway and worked at the Urology Department of Riks University, Oslo, Norway; Alice did not accompany him

1972   Attended the International Congress of Christian Physicians at York University, Canada, along with Alice in 1972; then they visited the USA as guests of Dr. and Mrs. Kristofer Hagen

1978	Visited Norway and Denmark along with Alice in 1978; also attended the International Congress of Christian Physicians at Davos, Switzerland
1988	Honoured with the Paul Harrison Award by CMC, Vellore, in 1988
1989	Contested the Shikaripara state assembly seat in 1989 as the Congress Party candidate; lost to Nalin Soren of JMM
1998	Retired from the post of Medical Superintendent in April 1998 but got extension and continued to work as a Senior Consultant at the Hospital; invited as a Special Guest by the CMC Vellore Alumni Association, USA Chapter, to their gathering at Philadelphia, USA, in May 1998; was accompanied by Alice
2001	Retired from Mohulpahari Christian Hospital in March 2001 and started working at his son's clinic in Dumka; Alice retired from the post of Principal but continues as an Honorary Consultant at the Nursing School
2002	Passed away after cardiac failure on 8 January, 2002, at Mohulpahari Christian Hospital; was buried at Mohulpahari

Two Speeches of

Dr. Stephen B. Hansdak

Delivered at Split Rock Resort,

Philadelphia, USA,

At the CMC Vellore

Alumni Association Meeting,

USA Chapter, May 1998.

First Speech

Mr. Chairman, my dear classmates and their family members, other CMC Vellore alumni and their family members and friends, today I am very happy to be here with you. First of all, my wife and I thank you, my classmates, who have invited us and paid for our trip here. We thank all of you who have come here to the Alumni meeting.

In the beginning, I want to remind you that I have rarely spoken English after leaving Vellore. Our main languages are my native Santali, then Hindi and Bengali. So, if I can't express myself very well, please excuse me.

I want to tell you about my people, their medical traditions and the impact of modern medicine on them. We come from the Santal tribe whose population is nearly 50 lakhs, and spread over Bihar, West Bengal, Assam, Orissa, Madhya Pradesh, Nepal and Bangladesh. Santals are the largest tribal group in India.[1] Santals have very clear and distinctive laws and customs, which they still practice. But some bad customs are being abandoned gradually.

Let me begin with my struggles in life and how I became a doctor. I am the seventh child in a family of ten children. My father was a primary school teacher and a small farmer. My grandfather had become a Christian in a peculiar way. His wife, my grandmother, was thought to be a witch and hence the people of their village planned to kill her.[2] One night, my grandfather and grandmother ran away from their village and took shelter under a Norwegian missionary. They then decided to become Christians. Later, my grandfather became a pastor of the Santal Mission.

We were very poor and did not have enough to eat. Yet my parents sent all of us to the local school to study. In my childhood, I used to look after the cows and goats of the family, besides studying in school. After finishing class III, I was sent to a boarding school at Kaerabani.[3] There I used to wash the clothes and plates of the senior students. In return, they allowed me to wash my dirty clothes with their soap, since I could not afford to buy soap.

I was good at studies, so I got scholarship every year. My father paid part of our boarding fees with vegetables that he grew on his farm and sold to our hostel. In this way, I completed high school. I got First Division in the Matriculation Examination. I also took part in sports and became School Champion in sports for two consecutive years.

Our Principal was an American missionary named Rev. Harold Riber. He noticed my good performance and advised me to study Science with Biology, so that I could become a doctor. I told him that my father could not afford to send me to college. Then the Principal said that the Santal Mission would give me scholarship to study Science and send me to Vellore for medical studies.[4] I had never heard of Vellore! In fact, I had never travelled in a train!

I went to Ranchi for Intermediate in Science, which I completed in 1954. That year I was late in applying for CMC, Vellore. So I taught Science in my old school for one year. In 1955, I applied for the MBBS course at CMC, Vellore, but in the final interview I did not pass because I could not speak English.[5]

I was asked to go to CMC, Ludhiana, but I had not applied there. The missionaries strongly recommended me for admission since there were no Santal doctors in my Church at that time. So the selectors reluctantly selected me for admission. The Registrar, Dr. J.C. David, told the selectors that even if Stephen did not pass MBBS in five years and took seven or eight years, at least the Santal Mission would have one native doctor. He called me and told me that he had persuaded the Selection Committee to select me even after my failure. He asked me to study hard from the beginning. So I attended all the classes, took down good notes and studied hard every day. Gradually I learnt to speak English and a few people became friendly with me.

In the First Final Examination, I got top marks in Physiology and created a sensation among the selectors. Dr. J.C. David was very proud of me. He phoned all the selectors and boasted that he had selected me, who had turned out to be a good student. From that time onwards, all my classmates became friendlier towards me and I too learnt to speak English properly.

☆ ☆ ☆

After internship, I joined Mohulpahari Christian Hospital in May 1961. Our Medical Superintendent was an American doctor named Dr. Kristofer Hagen who was an 'all rounder' as a doctor and a strict disciplinarian. I learnt many things from him but I wanted to study further. Like all of you, I too planned to go to USA and passed the ECFMG Examination in 1963.[6] Instead, an MS seat was arranged for me in Vellore. By then, I had two children so family support scholarship was also arranged for us for three years. After getting my MS degree, I returned to Mohulpahari in 1968.

The salary in our mission hospital was very small. Both my wife and I worked hard yet we could not manage our expenses properly because we had to support our aging parents, and our younger brothers and sisters too. So we started to grow our own rice and vegetables.

After hospital work, both of us worked in our large kitchen-garden to grow vegetables. We also got land on mortgage for rice cultivation. We got servants to work in our fields and we supervised them during our free time. In this way, we managed our family. After completing our post graduation studies in Vellore, we continued to work part-time as rice and vegetable cultivators. Thus, we saved money for our children's education in a good English-medium boarding school, which was some 300 kilometers away from our rural hospital.

I completed MS in General Surgery in three years' time. By God's grace, I passed in the first attempt. I remember Dr. A.S. Fenn, who was then Head of the Department of Surgery, came to my house at noon when I was eating lunch. I was very scared as to why he had come to my house. Then he said to me, "Don't be afraid, I have good news for you. You have passed M.S." He asked me how I had managed to pass so easily. I replied that I depended on God fully and did my duty properly. If God wanted me to go back to our mission hospital, He would certainly help me to pass.

In Vellore, I learnt to trust in God and accepted Jesus Christ as my personal Saviour and Master. As a result, my life became disciplined. I lived without much worry and fully trusted in God. I accepted Dr. Ida Scudder's motto: *"Not to be ministered unto but to minister"*. Thus, I lived in a small mission hospital, fully satisfied. I found joy in my work and in helping my own people.

The Santal people are hunters and cultivators. The same blood runs in me. In Mohulpahari, I used to go hunting and fishing very often. In those days, there was no prohibition on hunting or shooting of leopards since they were found in plenty. I will tell you about my first leopard-shooting in 1962. One day, some villagers from a nearby village came and told me that a big leopard had killed a cow in the jungle that day, but could not eat it since the cowherds had chased it away. They asked me to shoot it since the senior doctor, who had a gun, was away. So I borrowed a gun and a few cartridges, and went to the site with two of my friends. We made an enclosure with four *charpoys* (string cots) which we covered with fresh leaves and branches. We sat inside it, some 15-20 feet away from the carcass.

At about 5 p.m., the leopard descended on the carcass after all the people had left. I shot it in the chest but it did not die instantly. It roared and leaped about and bit off the branches of trees, for about twenty minutes. By then, it had become darker and rain had started falling. The leopard finally became silent. But we did not know whether it had died or run away. We were very, very afraid. We trembled inside our enclosure and prayed silently to God. In fact, one of my friends was trembling vigorously. When we are in danger, we remember God. This is the way with all human beings.

Since it was getting dark, we retreated from the back of the enclosure and told the villagers not to go near that place till we returned next morning. But the villagers did not wait for us. They had already collected the dead leopard and brought it to the village by the time we came. Later, I shot four more leopards which had been killing cows and goats.[7]

Similarly, I have had many interesting fishing experiences. On Sundays and other holidays, we often go fishing to fresh water ponds and lakes. In one of our mission stations, there is a pond with big fishes. Many of us spend our holidays there with our fishing rods.

One hot afternoon, I was sitting with my rod near this pond, wearing only a *lungi* (sarong) over my underwear. My wife was sitting nearby with some women. Suddenly, a big fish took the bait and started pulling away. I pulled my rod but the fish was much stronger and dragged me into the water. I did not leave my rod. Other people helped me to pull the fish. In the pressure and confusion, my *lungi* fell down into the water and I only had my underwear. Nobody noticed this, including myself. Then all the people on the bank started laughing very much. My wife came, got my *lungi* and tied it around me. And I got the fish.

In this way, sports and games keep us cheerful. We also have football games in many villages. Our hospital has a good team of players and we have played in many tournaments.

★ ★ ★

I have been very active in church work too. I have preached in our local Church and in other places, whenever I was called to do so. I have been chosen Congregation Elder and elected to the Diocesan Council and the Synod, for several terms. At present, I am the Chairman of the Constitution Revision Committee of our Church.

In the hospital, I am now a Consultant. After my retirement from the post of Medical Superintendent in April 1998, I have been working only four days a week in the hospital.

In 1988, I was awarded the Paul Harrison Award by CMC, Vellore. Although it was difficult to work all my life in a rural hospital, I have found it very satisfying.

Financially, there was not much gain but, mentally and spiritually, there has been job satisfaction and God's blessing.

I used to be worried about my children's education but God has provided everything for us. All my children are well-educated and well-settled in life. Now I can say that everything works out for good for them that love God.

Second Speech

Our Church was originally started by Norwegian and Danish missionaries in 1867. Later, after 1945, the Americans also joined in the mission work. This Mission was called the Santal Mission of the Northern Churches. There were 80,000 Christians in it, mostly Santals. There were also some Boros and Bengalis. The Church was spread over areas of Bihar, West Bengal and Assam. Some sister-churches of the Santal Mission were also started in Nepal and Bangladesh, among the Santals living there.

Since 1958, the local Church has become independent and is called the Northern Evangelical Lutheran Church or NELC. It runs its own affairs, with help from the original Santal Mission of Norway. Some mission societies of Denmark and USA also help us from time to time.

Our Church used to have four General Hospitals and two Leprosy Hospitals. Today, due to financial problems, only two General Hospitals are running. The others have been closed down. Similarly, one Leprosy Hospital in Assam has been closed down, while the other in Bihar has been handed over to the Leprosy Mission, which runs it today.

Mohulpahari Christian Hospital was started in 1951 by an American missionary doctor.[8] There was great need for hospitals and dispensaries in those days since the government did not provide much medical facilities, especially in the rural areas. So mission hospitals rendered medical help to many needy people. Nowadays, the government has also built a good infrastructure in rural areas through Primary Health Centres. However, due to lack of motivation and funds, this health service is not adequate. Therefore, private and mission hospitals still survive.

In our hospital, there are 130 beds with seven doctors, twenty-five staff nurses, and an attached nursing school for General (A-Grade) as well as ANM nurses. We see about 100 outpatients daily. We have three x-ray machines, one ultra sonogram machine, one upper GI Endoscope and one clinical laboratory. We do two or three surgeries daily. Our main specialty is general surgery but in a small hospital like Mohulpahari, we cannot have only one specialty. So I have to handle all work, such as general surgery, medicine, orthopedics, pediatrics, obstetrics & gynecology, and all the rest. We used open-drop ether anesthesia and spinal anesthesia in 1969-70. Now we use endo-tracheal anesthesia NO2, ether, etc. Patients come to me and say, "You are a surgeon trained in Vellore, so you must be able to do everything. We want to be operated by you." So I have to learn gynecological surgery, plastic surgery, urological surgery, etc. In an emergency, I have to manage head injury and open chest injury cases also.

I had learnt cleft lip and cleft palate correction surgery at CMC, Vellore, during my post-graduate training there. Earlier, congenital deformities like cleft lip and cleft palate were thought to be God-given and people did not come for surgery. One day, I saw some people with these deformities in the marketplace and told them that they could be corrected. In the beginning, I did some plastic surgery for free. When the patients got well, more people came.

In the early days, the Santal villagers treated doctors like gods. They did not blame the doctor if the patient died. They thought that the witches had eaten up the liver and lungs of the patient, so the doctor could not save him. The Hindus thought that it was the fate of the patient to die. So the doctor was not blamed. These people did not know anything about the Consumer Protection Act. But in the last ten years or so, people have become more aware and more demanding. No doctor has been prosecuted in our rural areas but it has happened in the large towns and cities.

Santals have their own herbal medicines and their medicine-men, who treat sick people with roots and herbs. Some are good and effective, but others can be harmful. These medicine men also work as witch-hunters. When a person is very ill, the relatives consult a medicine man. He rubs two *saal* leaves with oil and reads them. He then names a woman as being the witch who is eating the sick person. The villagers stone her to death or drive her out of the village. Today this bad custom has nearly come to an end due to the spread of education. Yet, even nowadays, some people will first try a medicine man. If his herbs don't work, they come to us.

The Santal villagers have great faith in the stethoscope. Only allopathic doctors use it, so they think that these doctors must be able to diagnose everything by listening to it. Sometimes people have asked me to use the stethoscope on their heads, legs and hands.

People are also very particular about food during their illness. They ask me what they should eat when ill. They name the food and ask if they should eat this or that. The Ayurvedic system gives much emphasis to diet. So people expect the same from us and we do not forget to prescribe the food for our patients.

People also have great faith in the injection. When they come to the hospital, they ask for injections. They think injections will work better.

Let me tell you about some of my early experiences. One day, soon after joining Mohulpahari Christian Hospital in 1961, I was called by the nurses in the Labour Room to deliver twins. The first baby came out normally but the second one would not. It was *transverse lie*. I did not know what to do. Then I remembered the ward teaching of our OB-Gyne teacher, Dr. Carol Jameson, at Vellore. She had said that, in such conditions, internal podalic version could be done and the baby delivered by breach. I tried it with great fear. Under light open-drop ether anesthesia, I put my hand through the cervix into the uterus, brought down the legs of the baby and delivered it. Both the mother and the baby were fine, but I nearly went into shock! Today, normal deliveries are usually conducted by our nurses in the Hospital. We also train village *dais* (midwives) for short periods of time and they take deliveries at home.

Another unusual experience I had was the case of a thirty-five year old man who was very emaciated, with a tumour in the right liver. He was diagnosed as a cancer patient in another hospital and sent to Mohulpahari. So I did surgery and removed a big mass from the ileocecal region. On biopsy, the tumour turned out to be TB caecum. The patient recovered and went back to join his work. But the senior officer would not allow him to join, saying he could not be the same person because that person had cancer and must be dead. Only after taking a certificate from us could he join.

Our major problems are these:

1. During the missionary era, most patients got free or concessional treatment in our hospital. Nowadays, we can't afford much concession. So all the poor people can't come to us.

2. We have no blood-bank in our hospital. We get blood from West Bengal, but it is very costly and not always available. So we get blood donors from the surrounding villages. We also ask the relatives of patients to donate blood.

3. We do not have specialty services like cardiology, pediatrics, cancer therapy, etc. So we refer patients to Calcutta or to Vellore.

4. We have problem retaining well-trained staff, especially doctors. There are no good schools in that area where the children of senior hospital staff can be sent for education. Their children usually go to boarding schools elsewhere.

5. We have the problem of increasing malaria and tuberculosis cases. During the last five years, we have noticed marked increase in malaria with cerebral complications. Sometimes, we have nearly 50% beds occupied by such patients. The treatment is expensive so many can't afford it. Similarly, lung tuberculosis also

appears to be increasing. This is due to growing resistance caused by incomplete treatment. More than 10% people in that area suffer from tuberculosis.

Luckily, we have not seen any AIDS patients in our hospital during the last three or four years. While screening, we got only two HIV positive patients. We have started educational programmes on STD, HIV and AIDS, where education is imparted to school children, villagers, teachers and other groups.

Overall, I have noticed good improvement in the economic condition and health status of the people over the last fifteen or twenty years. Similarly, more and more people are getting good education these days.

Explanatory Notes

[1] The indigenous/ tribal Santals (or Santhals) are also called *adivasis* in India (first dwellers). Today, they number about five million and are dispersed over a large area, mainly in the states of Jharkhand, West Bengal and Orissa; many have also migrated to Assam in North-East India, the Nepal foothills and northern Bangladesh. Santals call themselves *hor hopon* (children of men) as opposed to the *diku* (a non-tribal of the better class). According to modern anthropologists, the Santals belong to the Mundari group, which is Proto-Australoid and pre-Dravidian. They have a rich oral tradition and a strong sense of cultural identity.

[2] The Santal belief in witchcraft is closely linked to their oral tradition. According to an Ancestors' Story recorded by Rev. L.O. Skrefsrud, women tricked *Maran Buru* (the principal spirit of the Santals) into giving them the occult power of witchcraft. To take revenge on them, *Maran Buru* decided to give men the power of the *ojha* (witch-finder). The practice of witch-hunting is widely prevalent among other Jharkhand tribes too, such as the Munda, Oraon, Ho and Kharia. In a recent online article, Gladson Dungdung has described witch-hunting as a brutal form of violence practiced against women who are widows or who resist the patriarchal system, and then connects it with the destruction of the traditional land rights of tribal women. According to him, witch-hunting is on the rise in many adivasi-dominated villages of Jharkhand, with a police record of 984 women being killed in 19 districts between 1991 and 2008. Incidentally, the number of women killed for witchcraft in Dumka district is 11 as compared to 178 in West Singhbhum, 127 in

Lohardaga, 100 in Gumla, 60 in East Singhbhum, 60 in Palamu, 39 in Simdega and 34 in Saraikela-Kharsawan, among others. This discrepancy is explained by the fact that the land rights of Santal women were formally recognized at a meeting of the Santal *manjhis* and *parganas* at Dumka, in 1916. It was then recorded by Rev. P.O. Bodding and published as an Appendix in *The Traditions and Institutions of the Santals*. Today, this valuable book is considered to be the most reliable authority on Santal customary law. This law also gives rights to widows.

[3] Even before the arrival of the Scandinavian Lutherans, some schools had been started by the Church Missionary Society (CMS) for Santals in the late 1850s. The Santal Mission started its Boys' School in 1867, followed by the Girls' School in 1868, both at Benagaria. The medium of instruction in them was partly Bengali and partly Santali. Skrefsrud worked as a teacher and prepared many of the school textbooks himself. In 1911, when Bengal was divided and the district of Santal Parganas came into existence in the new province of Bihar, the medium of instruction was changed to Hindi. In the same year, the Boys' School was shifted to Kaerabani while the Girls' School was shifted to Maharo. Skrefsrud was influenced by the CMS and oriented his teaching towards practical matters. He advocated the use of Santali as a medium of instruction and was convinced that the Roman alphabet was more amenable to the Santal students than the Bengali alphabet. Marine Carrin and Harald Tambs-Lyche have pointed out that both Skrefsrud and Boerresen disliked boys who tried to put on Bengali manners, clothes or shoes. They add that the question of teaching in English had been vetoed by Skrefsrud in the 1870s because he feared that its introduction would turn the boys into "preposterous clowns".

[4] The Christian Medical College, Vellore, or simply CMC, Vellore, has acquired an iconic status in India's Christian medical history. Its unique vision began with Dr. Ida S. Scudder, who opened a one-bed clinic at Vellore in 1900. Two years later, in 1902, she built a 40-bed hospital. In 1909, she started the School of Nursing and in 1918, the Christian Medical College or CMC, which initially provided medical training only to women. Men were admitted after 1947. Besides training Indian women as health care professionals, CMC, Vellore, also brings medical care to the poor and the disabled of rural India through its internationally-acclaimed roadside dispensaries.

[5] Dr. Hansdak's awareness of English as the new language of power in independent India was learned during his early years at

CMC, Vellore. It is interesting to note that he refused to send his children to the Hindi-medium schools run by the Santal Mission at Kaerabani and Maharo. Instead, he sent them to expensive convent schools run by the Roman Catholics in urban areas. Dr. Hansdak's refusal to send his children to the local mission schools was frowned upon by many missionaries who, like Skrefsrud, believed in the use of Hindi and Santali for school instruction. Today, this prejudice against English-medium education for Santals is gone and the NELC even runs an English-medium high school at Dumka. Hence, Dr. Hansdak proved himself ahead of his time.

[6] The Educational Commission for Foreign Medical Graduates or ECFMG was and still is an examination for international medical graduates to enter residency or fellowship in the United States. It is accredited by the Accreditation Council for Graduate Medical Education (ACGME).

[7] Earlier, the forests of the Santal Parganas had been home to wildlife such as leopards, black bears, foxes and peacocks. By the mid-1980s, there was severe deforestation while the wildlife disappeared entirely. The arrival of modern firearms exterminated the wildlife while a corrupt administrative system destroyed its lush forests. Santals venerate the *sarjom* (*saal* tree) which forms their *jaher* (sacred grove). Sadly, the sturdy *sarjom* wood has been smuggled by corrupt forest guards and officials, in league with timber merchants. So while Santal villagers are often jailed for cutting trees, the Forest Department is the real culprit.

[8] Medical work by the Santal Mission started with the arrival of a Danish missionary couple named Dr. and Mrs. Johansen at Benagaria in 1902. However, due to illness and other reasons, they had to return to Denmark after only ten months. In 1915, Dr. Christine Larsen and Dr. B.B. Borg arrived from Denmark. While Dr. Larsen took up medical work at Dumka and Maharo, Dr. Borg worked at Benagaria. In 1923, Dr. Larsen married Rev. P.O. Bodding and moved to Mohulpahari, where she ran a small hospital from 1923 to 1934. After the Boddings left India in 1934, the hospital at Mohulpahari was closed down. As for the hospital at Benagaria, Dr. Borg carried on the work there from 1915 to 1928. A Bengali Christian doctor named Dr. Banerjee also joined the Benagaria hospital in 1921 and worked there for many years. In 1928, a new hospital was dedicated at Benagaria just before Dr. Borg left India.

His work was taken over by an American doctor named Dr. Erling Ostergaard. In 1946, after the end of the Second World War, many American doctors and nurses arrived at Benagaria. Among them were Dr. and Mrs. Kristofer Hagen, Ms. Alice Axelson and Ms. Hilma Gjerde. In 1949, Dr. Hagen decided to move the 60-bed hospital from Benagaria to Mohulpahari. Consequently, a new 90-bed hospital called the Mohulpahari Christian Hospital was dedicated on February 18, 1951 at Mohulpahari, with Dr. Kristofer Hagen as its first Medical Superintendent. In 1952, Dr and Mrs. Hagen left India on furlough and Dr. Otto Forman from Denmark became the next Medical Superintendent. After him came Dr. William R. Scott from the USA in 1955. Dr. Scott was the Medical Superintendent till 1960, when Dr. Hagen returned from furlough and started his second stint as the Medical Superintendent. Finally, Dr. Hagen left India in 1962 and was succeeded by Dr. Egil Ofstad from Norway. He left India in 1964, when Dr. Scott returned on his second stint and took over as Medical Superintendent. Dr. Scott left in 1967 and Ms. Alice Axelson, who was the Nursing School Principal, became the Acting Medical Superintendent till 1969. In May 1968, Dr. Stephen B. Hansdak returned from CMC, Vellore, with MS degree and became the Medical Superintendent in December 1969. He continued in this capacity till 1998, when Dr. Joyen Kisku took over as the Medical Superintendent. A Bengali Hindu doctor, Dr. B.B. Chatterjee, also served faithfully from 1933 until his death in 1973.

Bibliography

Books

Bodding, P.O. *A Santal Dictionary: 7 Parts in V Volumes*. New Delhi: Gyan Publishing   House, 2002.

Bodding, P.O., L.O. Skrefsrud and Sten Konow. *Traditions and Institutions of the Santals: Horkoren Mare Hapramko reak' Katha*, New Delhi: Bahumukhi Prakashan, 1994.

Carrin, Marine and Harald Tambs-Lyche. *An Encounter of Peripheries: Santals, Missionaries and their Changing Worlds, 1867-1900*. New Delhi: Manohar, 2008.

Doerdal, Elizabeth. *Paul Olaf Bodding: His Call and His Service*. Dumka: Sharda Press, 2007.

Hagen, Kristofer. *Third World Encounters: Dreams of Development*. Maple Grove, MN: Nystrom Publishing Company, 1984.

Hodne, Olav. *L.O. Skrefsrud: Missionary and Social Reformer among the Santals of Santal Parganas*. Oslo: Forlaget Land Og Kirke, 1966.

___________, *The Seed Bore Fruit: A Short History of the Santal Mission of the Northern Churches, 1867-1967*. Calcutta: C.D. Media, 1982.

Kumar, Raj. *Dalit Personal Narratives: Reading Caste, Nation and Identity*. New Delhi: Orient Blackswan, 2010.

Articles

Hansdak, Dr. S.B. "A Short History of Mohulpahari Christian Hospital", *Mohulpahari Christian Hospital: 1950-2000: Golden Jubilee*, 2000, 8-9.

Hembrom, Ezichael. "Dr. Stephen B. Hansdak' ak' Jion Carit", *Jugsirijol*, July 2001, 3-5.

Other Sources

Dungdung, Gladson. "In the Name of Witch Hunting". *http:// joharadivasi.org/in-the- name-of-witch-hunting-by-gladson-dungdung/*

Mani, Mani M. "Hidden Gems of Vellore: Stephen B. Hansdak M.B.B.S; M.S". *http://www.vellorecmc.org/Gems% 20of%20 Vellore/Stephen%20Hansdak.htm*

Panji 2008. (Yearbook of the NELC, 2008).

About the Contributors

Anand Mahanand is Assistant Professor (Senior Scale), Department of Materials Production, English and Foreign Languages (EFL) University, Hyderabad, India.

Marine Carrin is Director of Research, CNRS, LISST, Centre of Anthropology, Toulouse, France.

Harald Tambs-Lyche is Professor of Social Anthropology, University of Picardie–Jules Verne, Amiens, France.